TRIBES of NATIVE AMERICA

Ojibway

edited by Marla Felkins Ryan
and Linda Schmittroth

BLACKBIRCH®
PRESS

THOMSON

GALE

San Diego • Detroit • New York • San Francisco • Cleveland
New Haven, Conn. • Waterville, Maine • London • Munich

THOMSON
™
GALE

LIBRARY OF CONGRESS CATALOGING-IN-PUBLICATION DATA

Ojibway / Marla Felkins Ryan, book editor ; Linda Schmittroth, book editor.
   v. cm. — (Tribes of Native America)
Includes bibliographical references and index.
Contents: Ojibway name — Origins and group affiliations — History — American settlers in Ojibway land — Customs — Daily life — Death and mourning — Current tribal issues.
 ISBN 1-56711-725-2 (alk. paper)
 1. Ojibwa Indians—History—Juvenile literature. 2. Ojibwa Indians—Social life and customs—Juvenile literature. [1. Ojibwa Indians. 2. Indians of North America.] I. Ryan, Marla Felkins. II. Schmittroth, Linda. III. Series.

E99.C6 O346 2003
973.004′973—dc21
2002015883

Printed in United States
10 9 8 7 6 5 4 3 2 1

Table of Contents

OJIBWAY

Name

Ojibway (pronounced *oh-jib-WAY*) means "puckered up." The name may come from the way the tribe's moccasins were sewn. The Ojibway's traditional name is Anishinaubeg, which means "first people." They are also known as Chippewa.

The Ojibway tribe's name may come from the way they sewed their moccasins.

Ojibway/Chippewa
Contemporary Communities

1. Saginaw Chippewa Indian Tribe
2. Sault Ste. Marie Tribe of Chippewa, Minnesota
3. Minnesota Chippewa Tribe (6 tribes)
4. Red Lake Band of Chippewa Indians
5. Wisconsin: 6 reservations
6. North Dakota: Turtle Mountain Band of Chippewa
7. Montana: Swan Creek and Black River Chippewa
8. Manitoba: 32 reserves
9. Ontario: 78 reserves
10. Saskatchewan: 13 reserves

Shaded area: Traditional lands of the Ojibway in Michigan's Upper Peninsula and Ontario.

Where are the traditional Ojibway lands?

The Ojibway lived north of Lake Huron and northeast of Lake Superior. Today, they live on about 25 American reservations. They also live in several provinces in Canada.

What has happened to the population?

French explorers thought there were about 35,000 Ojibway in the 1600s. Historians say there may have been two to three times more. In a 1990 population count by the U.S. Bureau of the Census, 103,826 people said they were Chippewa. About 60,000 Ojibway live in Canada.

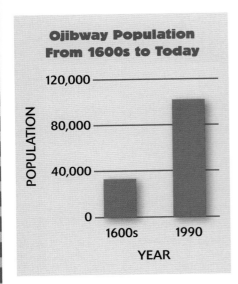

Ojibway Population From 1600s to Today

POPULATION

120,000

80,000

40,000

0

1600s   1990

YEAR

The Ojibway moved to the area surrounding Lake Superior around the year 900.

Origins and group ties

Ancestors of the Ojibway moved west from north of the St. Lawrence River to the Great Lakes region in about the year 900. After Europeans came, the Ojibway split into different groups. Some joined the Potawatomi and Ottawa in Michigan and Ontario. The Salteaux Ojibway lived in Michigan's Upper Peninsula. In about 1830, one group moved to the Great Plains. They became known as the Plains Ojibway, or Bungees.

The Ojibway made a huge group. They controlled the vast Great Lakes region for centuries. At one time, they may have been the most powerful tribe in North America.

Some Ojibway settled along the shores of Lake Huron (pictured), located on the boundary between present-day Michigan and Ontario.

HISTORY

An Ojibway story tells how their ancestors moved to the Great Lakes from a salt sea in the East—perhaps Hudson Bay. The people went through great hardship during their move, which took several hundred years.

Encounters with the French

When they first met Europeans, most Ojibway lived in the eastern part of Michigan's Upper Peninsula. Frenchman Etiénne Brulé came in 1622 to look for a waterway to the Orient.

The first Europeans the Ojibway met were the French. They established a good relationship and began trading goods.

Fur traders and missionaries came after French explorers. By the late 17th century, the Ojibway traded furs with the French. In return for animal skins, the tribe received guns and beads.

Once they had weapons, the Ojibway began to expand their lands. Between 1687 and the late 1700s, they pushed into what is now the Great Lakes region of the United States. They also moved into parts of Canada.

French pushed out by British

Between 1689 and 1760, France and England fought wars against each other in North America. The Ojibway sided with the French.

In 1760, France was defeated. This left the British in control of Ojibway lands in Canada. The British were angry because the Ojibway had helped the French. They did not allow the tribe to trade with them. The French also lost their influence in Michigan when the British defeated them in the French and Indian War (1755 to 1763).

American settlers in Ojibway land

The Ojibway took the British side in the American Revolution (1775 to 1783). They saw Americans as a greater threat than the British. After the British

1941
Bombing at Pearl Harbor forces United States into WWII

1945
WWII ends

1950s
Reservations no longer controlled by federal government

1968
Dennis Banks, George Mitchell, and Clyde Bellecourt found the American Indian Movement (AIM)

1983
The U.S. Court of Appeals rules that past treaties protect Ojibway rights to hunt, fish, and gather on their old lands

1988
The Indian Gaming Regulation Act lets the Ojibway open casinos on reservations

1989 to 1990
The National Museum of the American Indian Act and the Native American Grave Protection and Reparations Act bring about the return of burial remains to native tribes

Several Indian tribes, including the Ojibway, met with representatives of the American government to sign treaties that gave much of their land to white settlers.

lost the war, the Ojibway were made to sign treaties that gave much of their land to white settlers.

More migrations

Around 1830, many Ojibway moved to the plains. They became known as the Plains Ojibway, or Bungees. They lived in areas that are now North Dakota, northeastern Montana, and parts of Canada.

The Indian Removal Act was passed in 1830. It said that all Indians must move to Indian Territory (present-day Oklahoma and Kansas). Many Ojibway moved north to Canada instead. Some stayed behind. They tried to farm plots of land that the U.S.

government gave them under a plan known as allotment. Allotment was a way the United States tried to end the American Indian custom in which whole tribes, not individual people, owned the land. Those who took the small plots had to pay taxes. Often, the Ojibway could not pay. They had to sell their land to whites. During the 1860s, many Ojibway moved to Indian Territory with other tribes.

American Indian Movement founded

During the 20th century, American Indians and the U.S. government argued over issues such as forced removal and land use. The Red Power Movement, a series of protests, brought American Indian issues to the public eye. Then, in 1968, three Ojibway—Dennis Banks, George Mitchell, and Clyde Bellecourt—founded the American Indian Movement (AIM).

Dennis Banks (seated, second from right) co-founded the American Indian Movement in 1968.

In 1973, members of AIM stood guard at Wounded Knee, where a standoff with the government resulted in two deaths.

In 1973, AIM took over the village of Wounded Knee, South Dakota. There, Indians from many tribes tried to hold back U.S. forces in an armed standoff. Two Indians were killed, and many others were wounded. AIM's goal is to win civil rights for American Indians and to bring back tribal religion. The group also seeks to show how federal and state governments have broken treaties.

Religion

The Ojibway believed that the Creator, Kitche Manitou, made the world. First, the four elements—rock, water, fire, and wind—were formed. From these came the sun, the moon, the earth, and the stars. Next, plants grew. Then, animals and people were made.

The Ojibway see the sun as father and the earth as mother of all living things. The Ojibway feel they must care for and live in harmony with the earth. The *Midewiwin* was the Ojibway religious society. Members, who could be men or women, were called *Mides*. They went through a long training period. Their main job was to make life last longer. They were healers and also taught people how to behave.

In the 1600s, French Catholic missionaries tried to make the Ojibway Christian, with little success. This may have been in part because of the local Mides. Another reason may have been that the people lived in remote places that were hard to reach. Today, many Ojibway follow a religion that blends parts of their ancient beliefs with Christian beliefs.

An illustration on a piece of birch bark shows a seating plan for members of the Ojibway religious society, the *Midewiwin*.

This painting shows a French missionary preaching to Native Americans. The missionaries' efforts to convert the Ojibway were largely unsuccessful.

Government

In early days, the Ojibway were not highly organized. Small groups were spread over a wide area. Each group had its own tribal leader and council. Most leaders were men who had shown courage in battle or were wise and generous.

In 1934, the Indian Reorganization Act was passed. This law gave loans and other services to reservations if tribes made new constitutions and reorganized their governments. Most did so. Those tribes now have elected governing bodies.

Economy

The Ojibway were skilled fishermen and hunters. They knew how to gather nuts and berries. They also raised crops, such as squash and sunflowers, in a short growing season. After they met Europeans, the Ojibway began to trade with them.

The Ojibway were skilled hunters.

Today, some Ojibway on reservations harvest rice for a living.

Economy under U.S. government

On the reservations, the Ojibway sold their land and timber rights to earn money. That money was barely enough to live on. The people often had to rely on government welfare. Since the 1970s, however, legal cases have let the Ojibway use their land and lakes to support themselves.

At the end of World War II (1939 to 1945), most Ojibway moved to cities to find jobs. Today, they work in a wide range of jobs. Those on reservations often do seasonal work, such as forestry and harvesting wild rice. Since the 1970s, reservations have also run small businesses. Among these are bait shops, hotels, and restaurants.

Gambling

Many tribes have opened casinos. In Michigan and Minnesota, casinos bring in tens of millions of dollars and give jobs to thousands of Ojibway. Tribes have used some of this income to buy ancestral lands. They have also set up services, such as health and education.

DAILY LIFE

Families

The Ojibway worked hard to care for each other. They thought it was very important to share. The wealthy were supposed to share with those who had less. Though they worked hard, families found time to sew, carve, and make toys. They also told stories and played games.

Ojibway families made toys for their children.

Buildings

The traditional Ojibway home was the wigwam. It was made of birch bark or cattail mats that covered a pole frame. Twine or strips of leather tied the poles together. Sometimes, the Ojibway lived in tepees made of bark, buckskin, or cloth. The material stretched around a frame of poles that were tied together at the top.

Ojibway villages also had a sweat lodge. This building was used to cure illness or for people to cleanse themselves, often as part of a ceremony.

The Ojibway used a frame of poles covered with birch bark or cattail mats to make wigwams.

Native American women gathered wild rice and grew crops like corn and pumpkins.

Food

The Ojibway were mainly hunter-gatherers. Men used the bow and arrow and snares to hunt many kinds of game, including deer, mink, and rabbit. Strips of meat were smoked or dried to make a food called jerky. Dog meat was popular at feasts.

Women made maple syrup and maple sugar in the spring. Wild rice was harvested from rivers and lakes. If the weather was good, crops such as corn and pumpkins were grown in gardens.

Clothing

The Ojibway made clothing from cloth woven from nettle-stalk fiber and tanned hides. Green leaves covered the head in hot weather. Nettle-stalk cloth was used for women's underskirts. Hide was made into dresses, pants, and all kinds of garments. Animal skin or cattail down was worn on the chest

Ojibway kept their hair long and sometimes decorated it with paint or otter fur.

and inside moccasins in the winter. Small children wore hoods of deer hide with a flap that could be pulled forward to shade the eyes.

Earrings were worn mainly by old men. These could be made of fur, bone, or coins. Long ago, Ojibway men wore large nose rings and brass bracelets. The young men wore fur bands with beads around the wrists and ankles.

The Ojibway kept their hair long. Men usually wore braids. Men might put stripes of red and yellow paint on their hair. Women sometimes wound their hair in cloth or put it in two braids with a long row of otter fur over each braid.

Healing practices

The Ojibway thought people became ill if they upset supernatural beings. Illness might also come from social failure. For example, someone who did not host a feast after a good hunt might fall sick. Relatives carried a sick person to a healer's lodge. They also brought tobacco, which was seen as sacred, for the healer to smoke.

Most healers were members of the Midewiwin society. The healer might try to scare the patient to start the curing process. The healer might also sing. Ojibway healers knew about plants that could treat illnesses.

When Ojibway felt sick, they went to a healer (left).

Education

Children were seen as a gift to all the people. It was everyone's job to help bring them up well. To learn, children watched other people. It was considered very rude for them not to listen to others, especially elders. Children were taught to choose their words with care. They learned not to argue or make fun of others.

After the move to the reservations in the mid-1800s, the U.S. government took control of education. Children went to schools where they learned manual labor and how to care for a house. They were often taken away from their parents and were harshly punished if they did not follow the rules.

Today, most Ojibway children go to public schools. A few reservations, though, have preschools. There are also elementary schools and special classes that teach Ojibway culture, history, and language.

By the early 1900s, Ojibway children received formal schooling.

Arts

Music and dance are big parts of Ojibway ceremonies. Songs and dances often reflect nature. Many Ojibway elders were great storytellers. Ojibway stories have been kept alive by modern authors such as Ignatia Broker and Maude Kegg. Ojibway people in Michigan and Minnesota work to hold onto their culture. They sponsor arts and crafts shows and stage powwows (celebrations that feature songs and dances).

Ojibway danced in the opening ceremony for the tribe's annual powwow in Minnesota, in 1995.

NANABOZHO AND WINTER-MAKER

A character called Nanabozho appears in most Ojibway stories. He often gets into trouble, but he sometimes shows great cleverness when he outwits a natural or supernatural menace. Nanabozho teaches wisdom and medicine. He even tells animals how to hide from predators. This story offers an explanation for why winter comes and goes.

"Once upon a time this country was a big glacier. It was all ice and never was summer. The Indians lived here. They lived on and on.

One day Nanabozho came along. He said to the Indians, 'How are you going to keep on living in this snow and ice? There must be something we can do to make it more productive.' Nanabozho stirred them up.

The Indians then meditated. They made sacrifices and offerings, and fasted and prayed to the Great Spirit. They kept on meditating. They did not know what to do. They had been living comfortably before.

This problem was so great that they assembled again. They invited Nanabozho to sit in council at a feast to see what they could do about the great fear. When they were assembled, one old Indian, the wisest of the Ojibway, said, 'There is only one thing we can do. We shall have a feast of wild rice and wild roots and invite Old Man Winter—the Winter-Maker—to it. Nanabozho will be our scout. He knows where Old Man Winter is.' Nanabozho then prepared tobacco to take along to invite Old Winter-Maker-to the feast.

In an Ojibway story about the seasons, America is described as a big glacier.

Before the council began, the Indians huddled in secret. They planned to feed Old Man Winter a feast of boiling hot rice and herbs. They planned to keep him there and give him hotter and hotter food, so that he would grow fatter and sleepy, and sweat.

Finally Old Man Winter came. Oh, how the cold came when he came! Everything grew cold. The trees cracked and the forests cracked. The Indians kept on making the food hotter with hotter and hotter coals. Old Man Winter kept on eating and eating and growing warmer and warmer and perspiring more and more. At last, Old Man Winter said, 'You've got me. I believe I'll go.'

He walked out into the north and disappeared. When the Indians looked out, they saw green grass and fields and fruit trees and birds. But they heard Old Winter-Maker calling, 'I'm coming back; I'm coming back!'"

SOURCE: Coleman, Sister Bernard, Ellen Frogner, and Estelle Eich. *Ojibway Myths and Legends*. Minneapolis: Ross and Haines, 1962.

CUSTOMS

War and hunting rituals

Often before a war party set off, a ceremony called the Chief Dance was held. During the dance, the spirits were asked to protect the warriors. Tobacco and food were offered and a special drum was played.

When Ojibway hunters killed a bear, a ceremony was held. To show respect for the bear, its body was laid out and carefully cut up. Foods that bears like, such as maple sugar and berries, were placed next to the body. Everyone ate some bear meat. They promised the spirits that if another bear should come their way, it, too, would be treated with respect.

As part of a tribal ceremony, the Ojibway performed the Chief Dance and asked the spirits to protect their warriors.

Birth and naming

When a baby was born, guns were fired to let the village know. A rowdy feast was then held. It was believed that a lot of noise would make the child brave. Children had six names. The child was usually known by a nickname.

Puberty

The Ojibway had special rituals for boys and girls as they went through puberty. When a girl had her first menstrual period, she stayed for four days and nights in a small wigwam made for her by her mother. She did not eat and was told not to touch her body or face with her hands. After this, a feast was held in her honor.

Boys fasted and went on a vision quest. A boy's father took him into the woods and made a nest in a tree. The boy was left there for a few days, but the father checked on him now and then. Sometimes, a boy had to go through the ritual several times before he had a vision of his spirit guide. A feast was held when a boy killed his first game.

Ojibway children were usually called by a nickname.

Marriage

Ojibway people see themselves as part of their clan (a group of related families). A man had to marry a woman from another clan. Their children were part

Ojibway children became part of their father's clan.

of the father's clan. When a couple and the woman's parents agreed to a marriage, there was no formal wedding. The couple lived with the woman's family for a one-year trial period. If the marriage did not work out, or if the wife did not get pregnant, the man could go back to his parents. A couple who wished to stay together usually built their own lodge. They could also live with the man's family.

Couples could decide to separate. After a time, each person could marry again if they wished. Men might have more than one wife if he could afford to support them. Each woman would have her own part of his lodge. Some men named a head wife. She was the only one to have children. Ojibway were allowed to marry people who were not part of the tribe. By 1900, most Ojibway were of mixed heritage, most often French and Ojibway.

Death and mourning

The dead were dressed in their best clothing and wrapped in a blanket and birch bark. Sometimes the face, moccasins, and blanket were painted.

The body was removed from a wigwam through the west side and put into a grave. Also placed in the grave were food and other things the spirit would need for its trip to the afterworld. A close family member danced around the open grave. Then it was filled, and a funeral ceremony took place. Later, a bark house with a symbol of the dead person's clan was built over the grave.

Family members mourned for about a year. Special clothing was worn and a spirit bundle was made. It held a lock of the dead person's hair. A widow placed food in front of her husband's spirit bundle. She also slept with the bundle. When a baby died, the mother carried the child's clothes on a cradle-board (a board that babies are strapped onto) for a year. A mourner's ceremony was held once a year. During it, mourners were comforted and given gifts. After that, loved ones ended their mourning period and joined the community again.

An Ojibway family mourned a death by making a spirit bundle that contained some hair from the person who died.

Today, Ojibway take an active role in issues that affect their tribe. In 1996, Ojibway men blocked a train carrying hazardous materials through their Michigan reservation.

Current tribal issues

Casino gambling on reservations is a big issue. Some say gambling helps tribal economies. Others say gambling money goes to just a few rich people including non-natives. They think the money does little to help the whole reservation.

Among the key issues the Ojibway face is the need for improved medical treatment. The tribe also strives to better manage natural resources and protect treaty rights. Better education is also important to the Ojibway.

Notable people

Jane Johnston Schoolcraft (1800 to 1841) was the daughter of a Scots-Irish fur trader and an Ojibway woman. She was one of the first American Indian women to publish poetry. Her poems described Ojibway culture.

The American Indian Movement (AIM) was founded by Ojibway Dennis Banks (1937–), George Mitchell and Clyde Bellecourt (1939–), in 1968. Leonard Peltier (1944–) also played a big role in AIM.

For More Information

Leonard Peltier is a member of the AIM.

Brill, Charles. *Red Lake Nation: Portraits of Ojibway Life.* Minneapolis: University of Minnesota Press, 1992.

Broker, Ignatia. *Night Flying Woman: An Ojibway Narrative.* St. Paul: Minnesota Historical Society Press, 1983.

Garte, Edna. *Circle of Life: Cultural Continuity in Ojibwe Crafts.* Duluth: St. Louis County Historical Museum, Chisholm Museum and Duluth Art Institute, 1984.

Johnston, Basil. *Ojibway Heritage.* New York: Columbia University Press, 1976.

Kegg, Maude. *Portage Lake: Memories of an Ojibwe Childhood.* Edmonton: University of Alberta Press, 1991.

Morriseau, Norval. *Legends of My People.* Ed. Selwyn Dewdney. Toronto: Ryerson Press, 1965.

Tanner, Helen Hornbeck. *The Ojibway.* New York: Chelsea House, 1992.

Vizenor, Gerald Robert. *The Everlasting Sky: New Voices from the People Named the Chippewa.* New York: Crowell-Collier Press, 1972.

Vizenor, Gerald Robert. *The People Named the Chippewa: Narrative Histories.* Minneapolis: University of Minnesota Press, 1984.

Glossary

Allotments individual pieces of land

Chippewa another name for Ojibway

Raid an attack on land or a settlement, usually to steal food and other goods

Reservation land set aside for Native Americans to live on

Ritual something that is a custom or done in a certain way

Treaty an agreement

Tribe a group of people who live together in a community

Index